$\mathcal{F}$AITH

Depending on God

9 studies
for individuals or groups

Dale & Sandy Larsen

With Notes for Leaders

InterVarsity Press
Downers Grove, Illinois

InterVarsity Press
P.O. Box 1400, Downers Grove, IL 60515-1426
World Wide Web: www.ivpress.com
E-mail: mail@ivpress.com

InterVarsity Press® is the book-publishing division of InterVarsity Christian Fellowship/USA®, a student movement active on campus at hundreds of universities, colleges and schools of nursing in the United States of America, and a member movement of the International Fellowship of Evangelical Students. For information about local and regional activities, write Public Relations Dept., InterVarsity Christian Fellowship/USA, 6400 Schroeder Rd., P.O. Box 7895, Madison, WI 53707-7895, or visit the IVCF website at <www.ivcf.org>.

LifeGuide® is a registered trademark of InterVarsity Christian Fellowship.

Cover image: Bill Hatcher/National Geographic Society

ISBN 0-8308-3081-2

Printed in the United States of America ∞

P	17	16	15	14	13	12	11	10	9	8	7	6	5	4
Y	16	15	14	13	12	11	10	09	08	07	06	05		

Contents

GETTING THE MOST OUT OF *FAITH* ———————— 5

1 **In Praise of Faith**   Hebrews 11:1-16 ——— 9

2 **Abraham**
Faith Under Construction   Genesis 12:1-9 ——— 13

3 **Righteousness by Faith**   Romans 3:19-26 ——— 18

4 **Naaman**
Faith Without Fireworks   2 Kings 5:1-15 ——— 22

5 **Faith Without Action**   James 2:14-26 ——— 27

6 **David**
Faith That Worships   2 Samuel 7:18-29 ——— 31

7 **The Focus of Faith**   Hebrews 12:1-11 ——— 35

8 **In Jesus' Name**
Faith That Asks   John 16:16-28 ——— 39

9 **The Finale of Faith**   2 Timothy 4:6-18 ——— 43

Leader's Notes ————————————— 47

Getting the Most Out of *Faith*

"I've prayed for this one thing for years, and it hasn't happened. The Bible says all things are possible for the one who believes. What's wrong with my faith?"

"Some days it's easy for me to trust the Lord. Other days, no matter how hard I try, I don't feel confident that God cares or will help me. Or I forget God, go my own way and try to run my own life. How can my faith be more consistent?"

"All the indicators say that I don't have a chance at getting this job. But I'm still praying that I get it. Won't the Lord honor my faith?"

"I'm in a very unpleasant situation. Should I boldly pray that it changes? Or should I stick it out and trust God to bring good out of it? Which one is faith?"

"Our church stepped out on faith and started a building program, and now we're sunk in debt. Were we wrong to commit ourselves to the program? Or did it fail because our faith faltered?"

If you ever struggle with these or similar uncertainties about faith, you'll find good company in the pages of the Bible. All through the Scriptures we see people's faith in God knocking against the realities of earthly life—sometimes joyfully, sometimes desperately. There are many surprises. Some of the most esteemed biblical people let us down midstory when they apparently abandon their trust in God. And some of the least likely people, pressed by crisis, show remarkable outbursts of pure faith in a God they barely know.

Because faith presupposes an unseen world where unpredictable things happen, it always has an element of the mystical. But no longer is *faith* a stained-glass word tied to religious liturgy or doctrine. Even the secular world tells us that if we have faith in ourselves, we can accomplish anything. Physicians agree that faith—any faith—helps people cope with illness, and sometimes it brings unexplainable recovery.

So does it matter what we believe, so long as we believe in something?

Scripture says yes, it matters a great deal what or who we choose to believe. Biblical faith is not a free-floating positive feeling within myself. It is trust in a person outside of, other than and infinitely greater than myself.

The following nine Bible studies alternate between studies of people and studies of faith's essence as taught by faithful people. We'll meet Abraham, Naaman, David and Paul, imperfect people whose faith grew through testing. We'll see Jesus, both the perfect model of faith and the One who invites us to have faith in him. We'll consider faith's "hall of fame," the gift of forgiveness through faith in Christ, faithful action and faith's rightful focus.

Don't let questions discourage your faith. Our human faith will always be faltering and imperfect. But like a parent teaching a child to take the first steps, God welcomes and encourages the smallest step of trust toward himself. By God's grace we are being made into ever more faithful people. Our prayer is that this LifeGuide study will be part of that process.

Suggestions for Individual Study

1. As you begin each study, pray that God will speak to you through his Word.

2. Read the introduction to the study and respond to the personal reflection question or exercise. This is designed to help you focus on God and on the theme of the study.

3. Each study deals with a particular passage—so that you can delve into the author's meaning in that context. Read and reread the passage to be studied. The questions are written using the language of the New International Version, so you may wish to use that version of the Bible. The New Revised Standard Version is also recommended.

4. This is an inductive Bible study, designed to help you discover for yourself what Scripture is saying. The study includes three types of questions. *Observation* questions ask about the basic facts: who, what, when, where and how. *Interpretation* questions delve into the meaning of the passage. *Application* questions help you discover the implications of the text for growing in Christ. These three keys unlock the treasures of Scripture.

Write your answers to the questions in the spaces provided or in a personal journal. Writing can bring clarity and deeper understanding of yourself and of God's Word.

5. It might be good to have a Bible dictionary handy. Use it to look up any unfamiliar words, names or places.

6. Use the prayer suggestion to guide you in thanking God for what you have learned and to pray about the applications that have come to mind.

7. You may want to go on to the suggestion under "Now or Later," or you may want to use that idea for your next study.

Suggestions for Members of a Group Study

1. Come to the study prepared. Follow the suggestions for individual study mentioned above. You will find that careful preparation will greatly enrich your time spent in group discussion.

2. Be willing to participate in the discussion. The leader of your group will not be lecturing. Instead, he or she will be encouraging the members of the group to discuss what they have learned. The leader will be asking the questions that are found in this guide.

3. Stick to the topic being discussed. Your answers should be based on the verses which are the focus of the discussion and not on outside authorities such as commentaries or speakers. These studies focus on a particular passage of Scripture. Only rarely should you refer to other portions of the Bible. This allows for everyone to participate in in-depth study on equal ground.

4. Be sensitive to the other members of the group. Listen attentively when they describe what they have learned. You may be surprised by their insights! Each question assumes a variety of answers. Many questions do not have "right" answers, particularly questions that aim at meaning or application. Instead the questions push us to explore the passage more thoroughly.

When possible, link what you say to the comments of others. Also, be affirming whenever you can. This will encourage some of the more hesitant members of the group to participate.

5. Be careful not to dominate the discussion. We are sometimes so eager to express our thoughts that we leave too little opportunity for others to respond. By all means participate! But allow others to also.

6. Expect God to teach you through the passage being discussed and through the other members of the group. Pray that you will have an enjoyable and profitable time together, but also that as a result of the study you will find ways that you can take action individually and/or as a group.

7. Remember that anything said in the group is considered confidential and should not be discussed outside the group unless specific permission is given to do so.

8. If you are the group leader, you will find additional suggestions at the back of the guide.

1

In Praise of Faith

Hebrews 11:1-16

The runner who crosses the finish line first. The winning candidate on election night. The celebrity Oscar winner. All these get applause and congratulations.

But who cheers for the fired factory worker, leaving work for the last time, who still believes that God will provide for him and his family? Who throws confetti on the young woman, waking up in a hospital bed paralyzed from a car accident she can't even remember, who cries out to God for help instead of cursing him?

GROUP DISCUSSION. What do you think it means to live by faith? Who is someone you know that you would say lives that way?

PERSONAL REFLECTION. When have you wished you had more faith?

The Bible cheers for God's faithful people, and nowhere does the cheer sound more loudly and definitely than in the eleventh chapter of the book of Hebrews. The letter to the Hebrews was written by an unknown Christian to a group of persecuted Jewish Christians, people who needed to have their faith affirmed and strengthened. *Read Hebrews 11:1-16.*

1. Consider the actions of each of the people named in this passage. What does their behavior have in common?

2. If your name was one of those appearing in Hebrews 11, what do you think the writer would say about you?

3. Why do "the ancients" (the Old Testament faithful) deserve honor (vv. 1-2)?

4. How would you describe the faith for which they are honored?

5. Often we associate *faith* with feeling a certain way (for example: confident, bold, certain, doubt-free). What indicates that these people's behavior was based on something beyond emotional feeling (vv. 4-5, 7-9, 11)?

6. Do you typically need to feel full of faith before you can obey God? Give some examples.

7. In what ways did the faith of these people remain unfulfilled (vv. 13-16)?

8. How did they see themselves in relation to this world?

9. How does your faith in God affect your attitude toward this world?

10. In this passage, what connection do you see between faith and hope?

11. The writer takes great care to give his readers a full catalog of faithful people and the outcome of their faith. What does that indicate to you about the recipients of this letter? (Verses 1-16 are not the entire list; the names and honors continue through the end of the chapter.)

12. How would you define *faith?* (If your answer is only to repeat verse 1, rephrase it in your own words!)

13. How does Hebrews 11 encourage your own faith in God?

Thank God for the examples of faithful people. Pray that you will put into action the faith that you have, whether it is great or small.

Now or Later

Make notes about how you would like your attitudes to change during the course of this study on faith. Be as specific as possible.

2

Abraham

Faith Under Construction

Genesis 12:1-9

"Packing up, huh? Where are you headed?"

"I don't know. Well, I know the general area, but not the specific address."

"Oh. You got a job there?"

"Not exactly. In fact, not at all."

"What are you going to do when you get there?"

"I'm not sure."

"Really? Then why are you moving?"

"Because . . . God told me to." Such an answer is likely to bring a funny look. Some people would even question your mental stability. That was the situation of Abraham, Sarah and Lot as they set out from Haran to Canaan.

GROUP DISCUSSION. When have you made a major change because you believed the Lord wanted you to, and how did you know what God was asking you to do?

PERSONAL REFLECTION. How willing do you think you would be to make a major change in your life if God asked you to?

What factors would you consider?

In study 1 we visited Hebrews 11, the "hall of fame" of the Old Testament faithful. One of the prominent names is that of Abraham. *Read the beginnings of his story in Genesis 12:1-9.*

1. How did God break unexpectedly into Abram's (Abraham's) life?

2. We do not know how God spoke to Abraham or what form God took, but clearly it was a definite and understandable call. Put yourself in Abraham's place. What would you think?

What questions would you want to ask God?

3. How did God's promises cover many of Abraham's possible questions (vv. 1-3)?

4. How would Abraham's obedience affect the whole world (v. 3)?

5. What aspects of Abraham's situation would have compli-
cated his move (vv. 4-5)?

6. How have God's promises encouraged you to make a difficult change?

7. The group with Abraham and Sarah must have looked impres-
sive as they moved along the caravan route from Haran toward
Canaan (vv. 5-6). Trace their journey on a map in your Bible or
from some other resource. How do you think they would have
answered a traveler who asked, "Where are you going?"

8. A natural follow-up question to "Where are you going?" is
"Why?" How do you think Abraham and Sarah might have
answered?

9. Think of a major life change you have made or are in the process of making. If someone asked you, "Why are you doing this?" what would you say?

10. The land where God sent Abraham was occupied by the Canaanites, who were pagan worshipers of the nature god Baal (v. 6). How does Canaan resemble the setting of our life of faith?

11. When Abraham had traveled some distance into Canaan, what additional promise and encouragement did God provide (vv. 6-7)?

12. What do you notice about Abraham's response to this further revelation of the Lord (vv. 7-8)?

13. As he packed up and as he traveled, even when he arrived in Canaan, Abraham may have had doubts or questions about God's future fulfillment of his promises. Still Abraham kept acting in obedience. In what area of your life can you obey God in faith now, despite doubts or questions?

Thank God for how he has faithfully led and guided you and kept his promises.

No one can foresee the outcome of where following God may lead (except, ultimately, to heaven). Pray that you will obey God and go ahead to follow where he is leading you right now.

Now or Later

Abraham's knowledge of God deepened as he followed in obedience. Reflect on how your present knowledge of Jesus Christ compares with your knowledge when you first began to trust him? Consider not only facts you have learned but ways that he has showed you his character and has changed your character to be more like him.

In question 7 you used a map to trace Abraham's journey. Make a "map" to trace your spiritual journey so far. Note significant landmarks, milestones and even detours.

3

Righteousness by Faith

A sixth-grade boy had a troubled conscience. He confessed to his mother, "I told a lie. Will I still go to heaven?"

His mother answered, "You're only eleven years old. God is going to overlook that."

Was she right? It's a vital question because we all experience troubled consciences (and if we don't, we should!). If God overlooks a lie at age eleven, what about at age seventeen? Or thirty or forty? How *does* God deal with our wrongdoing? Does he keep score of good and bad and announce the totals when we die? Will he disregard all our sin because he loves us too much to hold anything against us?

GROUP DISCUSSION. Imagine that you are a judge. Someone you love is brought before you on trial. Which would you be more tempted to compromise: your justice or your love? Explain why you answer as you do.

PERSONAL REFLECTION. Suppose you are on trial for committing a serious crime, and you know you are guilty. Describe your thoughts and feelings. Now consider that Christ has declared you "not guilty," not because of a technicality or because you have a clever attorney, but because he has taken your penalty on himself. How do you feel?

We can speculate and wish about, and even fear, what God will do about our sin, but Scripture tells us what God has already done about it. In the first part of the book of Romans, Paul makes the case that both Jews and Gentiles are guilty under God's law and their own consciences. *Read Romans 3:19-26.*

1. What relationships do you see here between law, faith and righteousness?

2. In your own experience, what are some ways you have tried, or are tempted to try, to earn God's approval?

3. "The law" (v. 19) refers to God's law revealed in the Hebrew Scriptures, particularly the first five books of the Old Testament. God's law is expressed succinctly in the Ten Commandments. When we try to become acceptable to God by keeping his law, what is the "stone wall" or obstacle we keep running into (v. 20)?

4. If obedience to the law cannot make us righteous before God, what is the value of God's law (vv. 20-21)?

5. How does being "righteous" in God's sight differ from being a "good person" (that is, socially acceptable) (vv. 21-24)?

6. Why might it be easier, or at least seem easier, to work toward righteousness by being a good person than to accept God's righteousness in Christ?

7. What is God's part in our being justified before him (vv. 24-26)?

8. What is our part in being justified before God (vv. 22, 25-26)?

9. Paul's word *redemption* (v. 24) came from the contemporary slave market. It means "to buy someone out of slavery." From what types of slavery has Christ delivered us?

10. Many people agree with the mother in the introduction to this study. They hope that because God is loving, he will overlook sin. What light does this passage shed on that idea?

_____

11. If you are unsure, even occasionally, that God has forgiven your sins, what help and direction does this Scripture offer you?

_____

12. Think of someone you know who needs the message of this Scripture passage. How can you help that person understand Christ's forgiveness?

Thank God for his lavish gift of forgiveness in Christ. Thank him also that he does not leave us guessing about our forgiveness but grants us certainty.

Now or Later
Take notes of various ways people seek to connect with God. Stay on the lookout for evidence of spiritual searching as you watch TV, listen to music, read newspaper and magazines, and talk with people. Compare or contrast these attempts with what God has done in Jesus Christ and the response of faith. Consider how you can use people's efforts and longings as opportunities to share the gospel.

4

Naaman

Faith Without Fireworks

2 Kings 5:1-15

When Halley's comet passed by the earth in 1985, at least one person was disappointed. He said it wasn't like seventy-five years before, when he distinctly remembers hearing it go *"Whooosh!"* as it rushed past. In 1996 the comet Hyakutake passed closer to the earth than any comet in known history. Appearing as a blurry star, it disappointed those who expected a fiery display in the sky. When we tried to point out Hyakutake to some junior highers, they said "Yeah, sure, uh-huh," and got back in the car.

Our expectations of faith often resemble our expectations of comets. We hunger to see God do spectacular things. When instead God calls us to quiet acts of obedience, we say "Yeah, sure," and lose interest.

GROUP DISCUSSION. When have you been blessed by someone's very simple or quiet action?

PERSONAL REFLECTION. When you have physical needs, what kinds of responses show you that people care?

Identify some specific examples.

A Syrian army commander once sought help from the prophet Elisha. He expected a show, and he was disappointed—at first. *Read 2 Kings 5:1-15.*

1. Suppose you are Naaman. At which point in this story would you be most tempted to quit?

What would keep you going?

2. What is remarkable about the young servant girl's response to Naaman's leprosy (vv. 2-3)?

3. What approach did Naaman initially take toward getting his problem solved (vv. 4-6)?

4. How did the king of Israel's reaction complicate Naaman's quest for a cure (v. 7)?

5. Think of a time when your best efforts to find a solution to a problem were thwarted by another person. How did you feel and respond?

6. How did Elisha, the prophet, involve himself in Naaman's problem (vv. 8-10)?

7. How did Naaman react to Elisha, and why do you think his objection was so strong (vv. 11-12)?

8. When have you wished that God would do something dramatic in response to your faith?

9. How did Naaman's servants show wisdom (v. 13)?

10. Picture yourself as Naaman, as you begin to immerse your-self seven times in the Jordan River (v. 14). You go under and come up the first time, the second time . . . the sixth time . . . What are your fears and hopes?

11. Suppose you (as your real self; not as Naaman) were being advised by some people who have the wisdom of Naaman's ser-vants. What might they say to you right now?

12. Naaman was healed physically. What spiritual change took place within him as a result (v. 15)?

13. In what areas of your life do you think God waits for you to take a small step of obedience, so he can show you that he is truly God?

Ask God to open your eyes to the "small" things he does, which are actually big things in his sight. Ask him for courage to obey his promptings even if they seem trivial.

Now or Later

Consider areas of your life in which you need to obey as Naaman obeyed. Plan how you will you take the first step to "go down into the Jordan for the first time." Some possible examples:

• Cross an invisible barrier to talk to someone at church or in your neighborhood whom you have previously ignored.

• Vow to refrain from some harmful pattern, such as joining in gossip about coworkers.

Your obedience may bring no immediate visible results. You may not even feel better instantly. But consider how the step of getting to know a new person can lead to a friendship or to new attitudes toward people who are different. Think of how refusing to gossip can break a chain of half-truths or set a new kind of example at work.

5

Faith Without Action

Carl claimed to be a premier ballet dancer. He was also, he said, an accomplished hang-glider and champion ice skater. With such gold-plated credentials, why was Carl teaching ballet to a few students at a fitness center in a small town in Wisconsin? He was supposed to choreograph a musical for our local theater group, but he constantly changed the dances and confused his terminology, talking about "sixteen measures" when he meant "sixteen beats." After the musical, Carl disappeared from town. Maybe he's hang-gliding somewhere.

GROUP DISCUSSION. What is the biggest (and emptiest) boast you have ever heard?

PERSONAL REFLECTION. Have you ever bragged about something when it was not quite true? Why did you exaggerate?

Words! They're cheap. It is far easier to talk than to come up with actions to equal our words. James warned early Christian believers to match their words with action. His counsel still works for contemporary Christians. *Read James 2:14-26.*

1. According to James, what is the connection between faith and actions?

2. In what sense is faith without deeds lifeless (vv. 14-17)?

3. Describe some evidences of a dead faith.

4. When have you seen a gap between your own faith and your deeds?

5. What did you do (or are you doing) to bring the two together?

6. How does James answer the challenge that faith and works can exist independent of each other (v. 18)?

7. What surprising example does James use to show that "just believing" is not enough for saving faith (v. 19)?

8. How do the lives of Abraham and Rahab exemplify genuine faith in God (vv. 20-25)?

9. In verse 23, James quotes Genesis 15:6 concerning Abraham's faith. Paul quotes exactly the same Scripture in Romans 4:3 to show that we are saved by faith, not works. How can we reconcile these two ideas: that we are saved by faith and not deeds, and faith without deeds is dead?

10. In your own life where do you think people see evidences of authentic faith in Christ?

11. The book of James is a challenge for believers to mature in their faith. What are some areas where you need to expand your actions of faith?

12. What is one specific faith-action you will take this week?

Pray for genuine faith that does not stay private but makes itself known.

Now or Later

If you are doing this study in a group, name evidences of Christian faith that you see in each other. You may do this out loud or in written notes to give to each other.

If you are doing this study individually, write a note to someone expressing ways that you see that person's faith in action. Thank the person for the way he or she inspires your own faith.

6

David
Faith That Worships

2 Samuel 7:18-29

We planted a plum tree, an asparagus bed, raspberries and flowers. And then we decided to move. We knew the time was right, but to our neighbors it made no sense. Why do all that work and then hand it over to someone else before we had time to enjoy it?

King David made ambitious plans to build a temple for the Lord. The Lord showed him that the temple would indeed be built, not by him but by his son Solomon. David himself would never see the temple.

Faith is easy when everything goes as planned; disappointment severely tests our faith.

GROUP DISCUSSION. What do you usually do after a disappointment?

PERSONAL REFLECTION. What is a severe disappointment you have experienced? How did you respond? How did it affect your relationship with God?

Three thousand years ago, David became king of Israel and captured the stronghold of Jerusalem. Right away, he wanted to build a permanent temple to the Lord to replace the tabernacle, the movable tent that had been Israel's worship center since the time of Moses. In the first part of 2 Samuel 7, the Lord says through the prophet Nathan that the temple would not be built in David's time but would be built by his son. What follows is David's response to that news. *Read 2 Samuel 7:18-29.*

1. Think of three words or phrases that describe David's reaction to the news that his son would be the one to build the temple.

Which of these words or phrases could you apply to yourself when you receive disappointing news?

2. What makes King David's prayer worshipful?

3. David began his prayer with a question: "Who am I, O Sovereign LORD, and what is my family, that you have brought me this far?" (v. 18). What did he mean by this query?

4. When we have a strong sense of where we've come from and how far along the Lord has brought us, how is our faith affected?

5. David voiced awe that God had spoken of David's "house" (descendants) far into the future (vv. 19-21, 27). How is faith deepened by a vision of what the Lord can do beyond the here and now?

---

6. How did David express the unique privilege of belonging to God's people (vv. 22-24)?

---

7. In what ways have God's people inspired your own faith?

---

8. How is David's character revealed in what he requested and expected from the Lord (vv. 25-26, 29)?

---

9. Throughout this prayer, where do you find David's strongest expression of faith?

---

10. Why does faith in God lead naturally to worship of God?

11. When has a disappointment led you into worship, even if it took a while?

12. How can the union of faith with worship sustain you through troubled times?

Thank God that, in his wisdom, your life has not always worked out the way you planned.

Now or Later

In a spirit of worship, what would you like to say to the Lord about himself?

About yourself?

About how far he has brought you?

About your hopes for the future?

If you do this activity as part of a group, have a time of quiet reflection to consider and write your answers. Afterward, some group members may volunteer to read their prayers aloud. Let the spoken prayers lead you into a spirit of corporate worship. Later, commit yourself to spend time alone with the Lord in the next twenty-four hours, and read your answers aloud to him as a prayer.

7

The Focus of Faith

Hebrews 12:1-11

In the film *Chariots of Fire*, the sprinter Harold Abrahams loses a race because he keeps glancing sideways. Why? Because he is watching for his rival Eric Liddell. Afterward he berates himself for such amateur behavior. He's an Olympic-class runner, yet he broke a fundamental rule of racing: never look for the other runners.

GROUP DISCUSSION. When have you failed at a task because you were distracted?

PERSONAL REFLECTION. As you try to keep your focus on Christ, what most often distracts you?

In this session we pick back up on the text from study 1. *Therefore* (v. 1) refers to the faithfulness of the Old Testament people named in chapter 11. *Read Hebrews 12:1-11.*

1. Throughout this passage, what attitude does the writer urge us to take toward sin?

2. In what ways does your Christian life resemble a race?

3. What is the "race marked out for us" (v. 1)?

4. Why does keeping our eyes on Jesus help us to run with perseverance (vv. 1-3)?

5. Verse 2 says that Jesus is "the author and perfecter of our faith." The idea is that our faith depends on Jesus from beginning to end. How is Jesus involved in the beginning of our faith?

the continuation of our faith?

the culmination of our faith in heaven?

6. In our race of faith, how might we be distracted by the other runners?

by the track conditions?

by the cheers or boos of the crowd?

7. How is Jesus the perfect example of how we ought to run our own race of faith (vv. 2-3)?

8. Perhaps you have tried to be faithful to the Lord but still feel you are being punished for something. What help does this passage offer about how to respond (vv. 4-11)?

9. How does God's discipline demonstrate his love (vv. 6-9)?

10. What is the intended result of God's discipline (vv. 10-11)?

11. This coming week in your "race of faith," where do you anticipate the most danger of stumbling?

---

12. What strategies will you use to keep your focus on Christ?

Pray for endurance to continue to pursue Christ. Thank him that he is there at the beginning, middle and end—in fact at every step—of the race you must run.

Now or Later

Sketch yourself running with various "weights" of sin or other distractions. (Don't worry about the quality of your artwork.) You can picture the weights on your ankles, arms or head, in a backpack, or in any form that seems appropriate. Label each weight.

Now decide how you will cast off each weight this week. Make specific plans. To help remind you of your ultimate goal, draw a cross or some other representation of Christ as the goal of your running figure.

8

In Jesus' Name
Faith That Asks

John 16:16-28

Dale had been in the Army only a few months when he was assigned to the Chief of Staff's Office, Fourth Army Headquarters, Ft. Sam Houston. He was the lowliest private, with the job description of "courier": a high-sounding term for "office boy."

One day when Dale was leaving for his daily rounds, the secretary said that one of the generals wanted a particular classified document later that week, and would he check to see if it was in Transportation? In Transportation, Dale asked if they had the document. He also mentioned that General So-and-So wanted it.

He could hardly believe the effect of his words. Before he knew it, he had full colonels searching for that document. Because of his lowly private's status? Hardly. It was because Dale had asked in the name of General So-and-So.

GROUP DISCUSSION. When have you hesitated to ask for something because you felt you did not have enough status or clout? How did you get up enough nerve to ask (if you did)? What happened as a result?

PERSONAL REFLECTION. Would you say it is easier for you to ask the Lord for small things or big things? Why?

The text we are about to read reminds us that, when we pray with faith in the name of Jesus, the authority rests not in us but in the one who is in charge. This discussion takes place just after Jesus and the disciples have eaten the Last Supper. Jesus has encouraged the disciples with several promises: that he was going away to prepare a place for them, that he would send another Counselor to stay with them, and even that he and the Father would live within them. But not all his words were comforting. *Read John 16:16-28.*

---

1. What is the primary theme of Jesus' words?

---

2. Put yourself in that upper room as one of the disciples. Imagine the scent of the roasted Passover lamb, the sting of smoke from oil lamps, the power of Jesus' presence, the nagging fear that his enemies—and yours—are right outside. As you listen to Jesus' words, what is your mood?

---

3. Why were the disciples confused (vv. 16-18)?

4. How did Jesus respond to their apprehension (vv. 19-24)?

---

5. Childbirth seems an unusual illustration for Jesus to use when talking to an all-male group of disciples (vv. 20-22). How does childbirth illustrate what they were going to experience?

---

6. When have you felt the pain of the Lord's seeming absence?

---

7. The disciples' past experiences with Jesus (along with his constant reassurances) gave them something to "have faith in" for the uncertain future. What experiences in your past enable you to confidently pray with faith?

---

8. Jesus made it clear that asking in his name does not mean he asks the Father on our behalf (vv. 26-27). It also means more than just ending a prayer with the words "in Jesus' name, amen." What do you think he means by "ask in my name"?

9. What are the implications of verses 23-28 for a Christian's prayer life?

---

10. Why is joy a logical result of asking in Jesus' name (v. 24)?

---

11. How can we avoid misusing the privilege of asking in Jesus' name?

Thank the Lord that he allows us to freely approach him in prayer. Pray that your intentions will fit with his, so you can always pray "in Jesus' name."

Now or Later

What are some things you believe Jesus would have you ask for in the coming week?

in the coming year?

9

The Finale of Faith

2 Timothy 4:6-18

If you wander through an old graveyard, you'll notice that many tombstones have an epitaph, a saying that sums up the life of the deceased person. Most epitaphs are quite complimentary to the dead. *Spoon River Anthology* by Edgar Lee Masters is a collection of epitaphs with a twist. On each tombstone the deceased person finally tells the truth, beautiful or ugly, about his or her own life.

GROUP DISCUSSION. If your epitaph summed up your life of faith, what would it say? (Don't expect to give a complete answer off the top of your head, but come up with some possibilities.)

PERSONAL REFLECTION. If you could write your own epitaph, what would it say about your faith?

Paul's second letter to Timothy is probably the last letter he wrote. In that sense it is something like an extended epitaph for Paul. The apostle's last written words give us deep insight into his life of faith. *Read 2 Timothy 4:6-18.*

1. Throughout this passage, what clues do you get that these are Paul's last words to Timothy?

2. What does Paul's "life summary" (vv. 6-7, 16-17) tell us about what he considered essential?

3. How do Paul's essentials compare with your own?

4. From looking back on his life, Paul turned to looking forward. What was he confident about (vv. 8, 18)?

5. Notice who and what Paul asked Timothy to bring to him in prison (vv. 11, 13). How do his requests show his hope for a continuing ministry?

6. What emotions come through in Paul's account of his various relationships—good and bad (vv. 9-16)?

7. How had other people sometimes failed Paul (vv. 10, 14-16)?

8. How had the Lord helped Paul when people failed him (v. 17)?

9. How has the Lord helped you when people have failed you?

10. For what purpose was Paul's life preserved (vv. 17-18)?

11. What was Paul's ultimate hope?

12. Based on everything you have learned and discussed in this study, how would you like to revise the definition of faith that you wrote in study one?

Thank God for new insights into faith. Thank him also for remaining faithful to you even when your faith falters. Offer praise that Jesus is the one "on whom our faith depends from beginning to end" (Hebrews 12:1 TEV).

Now or Later
How would you like to change your "faith epitaph" from the group discussion or personal reflection?

How can you work toward that goal?

Leader's Notes

MY GRACE IS SUFFICIENT FOR YOU. (2 COR 12:9)

Leading a Bible discussion can be an enjoyable and rewarding experience. But it can also be *scary*—especially if you've never done it before. If this is your feeling, you're in good company. When God asked Moses to lead the Israelites out of Egypt, he replied, "O Lord, please send someone else to do it"! (Ex 4:13). It was the same with Solomon, Jeremiah and Timothy, but God helped these people in spite of their weaknesses, and he will help you as well.

You don't need to be an expert on the Bible or a trained teacher to lead a Bible discussion. The idea behind these inductive studies is that the leader guides group members to discover for themselves what the Bible has to say. This method of learning will allow group members to remember much more of what is said than a lecture would.

These studies are designed to be led easily. As a matter of fact, the flow of questions through the passage from observation to interpretation to application is so natural that you may feel that the studies lead themselves. This study guide is also flexible. You can use it with a variety of groups—student, professional, neighborhood or church groups. Each study takes forty-five to sixty minutes in a group setting.

There are some important facts to know about group dynamics and encouraging discussion. The suggestions listed below should enable you to effectively and enjoyably fulfill your role as leader.

Preparing for the Study

1. Ask God to help you understand and apply the passage in your own life. Unless this happens, you will not be prepared to lead others. Pray too for the various members of the group. Ask God to open your hearts to the message of his Word and motivate you to action.

2. Read the introduction to the entire guide to get an overview of the entire book and the issues which will be explored.

3. As you begin each study, read and reread the assigned Bible passage to familiarize yourself with it.

4. This study guide is based on the New International Version of the Bible. It will help you and the group if you use this translation as the basis for your study and discussion.

5. Carefully work through each question in the study. Spend time in meditation and reflection as you consider how to respond.

6. Write your thoughts and responses in the space provided in the study guide. This will help you to express your understanding of the passage clearly.

7. It might help to have a Bible dictionary handy. Use it to look up any unfamiliar words, names or places. (For additional help on how to study a passage, see chapter five of *How to Lead a LifeGuide® Bible Study*, InterVarsity Press.)

8. Consider how you can apply the Scripture to your life. Remember that the group will follow your lead in responding to the studies. They will not go any deeper than you do.

9. Once you have finished your own study of the passage, familiarize yourself with the leader's notes for the study you are leading. These are designed to help you in several ways. First, they tell you the purpose the study guide author had in mind when writing the study. Take time to think through how the study questions work together to accomplish that purpose. Second, the notes provide you with additional background information or suggestions on group dynamics for various questions. This information can be useful when people have difficulty understanding or answering a question. Third, the leader's notes can alert you to potential problems you may encounter during the study.

10. If you wish to remind yourself of anything mentioned in the leader's notes, make a note to yourself below that question in the study.

Leading the Study

1. Begin the study on time. Open with prayer, asking God to help the group to understand and apply the passage.

2. Be sure that everyone in your group has a study guide. Encourage the group to prepare beforehand for each discussion by reading the introduction to the guide and by working through the questions in the study.

3. At the beginning of your first time together, explain that these studies are meant to be discussions, not lectures. Encourage the members of the group to participate. However, do not put pressure on those who may be hesitant to speak during the first few sessions. You may want to suggest the following guidelines to your group.

☐ Stick to the topic being discussed.

☐ Your responses should be based on the verses which are the focus of the discussion and not on outside authorities such as commentaries or speakers.

☐ These studies focus on a particular passage of Scripture. Only rarely should you refer to other portions of the Bible. This allows for everyone to participate in in-depth study on equal ground.

☐ Anything said in the group is considered confidential and will not be discussed outside the group unless specific permission is given to do so.

☐ We will listen attentively to each other and provide time for each person present to talk.

☐ We will pray for each other.

4. Have a group member read the introduction at the beginning of the discussion.

5. Every session begins with a group discussion question. The question or activity is meant to be used before the passage is read. The question introduces the theme of the study and encourages group members to begin to open up. Encourage as many members as possible to participate, and be ready to get the discussion going with your own response.

This section is designed to reveal where our thoughts or feelings need to be transformed by Scripture. That is why it is especially important not to read the passage before the discussion question is asked. The passage will tend to color the honest reactions people would otherwise give because they are, of course, supposed to think the way the Bible does.

You may want to supplement the group discussion question with an ice-breaker to help people to get comfortable. See the community section of *Small Group Idea Book* for more ideas.

You also might want to use the personal reflection question with your group. Either allow a time of silence for people to respond individually or discuss it together.

6. Have a group member (or members if the passage is long) read aloud the passage to be studied. Then give people several minutes to read the passage again silently so that they can take it all in.

7. Question 1 will generally be an overview question designed to briefly survey the passage. Encourage the group to look at the whole passage, but try to avoid getting sidetracked by questions or issues that will be addressed later in the study.

8. As you ask the questions, keep in mind that they are designed to be used just as they are written. You may simply read them aloud. Or you may prefer to express them in your own words.

There may be times when it is appropriate to deviate from the study guide. For example, a question may have already been answered. If so, move on to the next question. Or someone may raise an important question not covered in the guide. Take time to discuss it, but try to keep the group from going off on tangents.

9. Avoid answering your own questions. If necessary, repeat or rephrase them until they are clearly understood. Or point out something you read in the leader's notes to clarify the context or meaning. An eager group quickly becomes passive and silent if they think the leader will do most of the talking.

10. Don't be afraid of silence. People may need time to think about the question before formulating their answers.

11. Don't be content with just one answer. Ask, "What do the rest of you think?" or "Anything else?" until several people have given answers to the question.

12. Acknowledge all contributions. Try to be affirming whenever possible. Never reject an answer. If it is clearly off-base, ask, "Which verse led you to that conclusion?" or again, "What do the rest of you think?"

13. Don't expect every answer to be addressed to you, even though this will probably happen at first. As group members become more at ease, they will begin to truly interact with each other. This is one sign of healthy discussion.

14. Don't be afraid of controversy. It can be very stimulating. If you don't resolve an issue completely, don't be frustrated. Move on and keep it in mind for later. A subsequent study may solve the problem.

15. Periodically summarize what the group has said about the passage. This helps to draw together the various ideas mentioned and gives continuity to the study. But don't preach.

16. At the end of the Bible discussion you may want to allow group members a time of quiet to work on an idea under "Now or Later." Then discuss what you experienced. Or you may want to encourage group members to work on these ideas between meetings. Give an opportunity during the session for people to talk about what they are learning.

17. Conclude your time together with conversational prayer, adapting the prayer suggestion at the end of the study to your group. Ask for God's help in following through on the commitments you've made.

18. End on time.

Many more suggestions and helps are found in *How to Lead a LifeGuide® Bible Study*.

Components of Small Groups

A healthy small group should do more than study the Bible. There are four components to consider as you structure your time together.

Nurture. Small groups help us to grow in our knowledge and love of God. Bible study is the key to making this happen and is the foundation of your small group.

Community. Small groups are a great place to develop deep friendships with other Christians. Allow time for informal interaction before and after each study. Plan activities and games that will help you get to know each other. Spend time having fun together—going on a picnic or cooking dinner together.

Worship and prayer. Your study will be enhanced by spending time praising God together in prayer or song. Pray for each other's needs—and keep track of how God is answering prayer in your group. Ask God to help you to apply what you are learning in your study.

Outreach. Reaching out to others can be a practical way of applying what you are learning, and it will keep your group from becoming self-focused. Host a series of evangelistic discussions for your friends or neighbors. Clean up the yard of an elderly friend. Serve at a soup kitchen together, or spend a day working on a Habitat house.

Many more suggestions and helps in each of these areas are found in *Small Group Idea Book.* Information on building a small group can be found in *Small Group Leaders' Handbook* and *The Big Book on Small Groups* (both from InterVarsity Press). Reading through one of these books would be worth your time.

Study 1. In Praise of Faith. Hebrews 11:1-16.

Purpose: To begin to consider what faith is and to survey some Old Testament examples of strong faith.

Question 1. All these people put the reality of God ahead of this physical, tangible world, and they acted accordingly. For some, faith meant they took daring risks. For others, faith meant they waited or simply lived daily in a way that would please God.

Question 2. This question may be met with silence at first. Most group members will be reluctant (and should be!) to place themselves in such a list along with the Old Testament heroes of the faith. You may want to rephrase the question something like this: "If someone were to write a short statement in honor of your faith in God, what might the writer say?" The point of the question is not to directly compare ourselves with the biblical people but to consider the outcome of faith. Be prepared with your own response, and offer it as an example if no one comes up with an answer after a minute or so.

Questions 3-4. "To the writer to the Hebrews faith is a hope that is absolutely certain that what it believes is true, and that what it expects will come. It is not the hope which looks forward with wistful longing; it is the hope which looks forward with utter certainty. It is not the hope which takes refuge in a perhaps; it is the hope which is founded on a conviction. In the early days of persecution they brought a humble Christian before the judges. He told them that nothing they could do could shake him because he believed that, if he was true to God, God would be true to him. 'Do you really think,' asked the judge, 'that the like of you will go to God and His glory?' 'I do not think,' said the man, 'I know' " (William Barclay, *The Letter to the Hebrews,* 2nd ed. [Philadelphia: Westminster Press, 1957], pp. 144-45). If you and the members of your group are not at a point of such absolute certainty in your faith, don't despair. Take Hebrews 11:1 and Barclay's comments as your ideal as you grow in faith together.

Question 5. Throughout the Bible, faith is different from optimism or wishful thinking. It is trust in something—or rather in Someone. Faith is often accompanied by an inner feeling of confidence, but not necessarily all the time. Scripture usually does not tell us how the people in Hebrews 11 felt about their circumstances. We do know that when God acted upon them or spoke to them, from outside themselves, they responded. Abel was commended by God; Enoch was taken from the earth without dying; Noah was warned and saved his family; Abraham was called and was miraculously enabled to become a father. Often the evidence that God would help or would prove true was not there until after they took obedient action.

Question 7. "All the believers mentioned in this passage were to be the living stones of foundation upon which others would be laid. Thus they would be completed in those who would come later. We who have come later are those completing stones, giving the saints of old the joy and satisfaction realized by any pioneers who are able to look back and see their dreams fulfilled in later generations" (Louis H. Evans Jr., *The Communicator's Commentary: Hebrews* [Waco, Tex.: Word, 1985], p. 204).

Question 11. The recipients of this letter needed clear examples of strong faith which stood firm under testing. We can conclude that they were being tested themselves. From other places in Hebrews we gather evidence of persecution (10:32-34; 13:23). "The readers are obviously predominantly Jewish and are under pressure to give up their Christian distinctives (either from the synagogue or from Gentile persecution of Christians)" (Craig S. Keener, "Introduction to Hebrews," in *The IVP Bible Background Commentary: New Testament* [Downers Grove, Ill.: InterVarsity Press, 1993], p. 648).

Question 12. At the end of the group's nine weeks of study, you will look back at your definitions and consider how your concept of faith has changed and how it has been confirmed.

Study 2. Abraham: Faith Under Construction. Genesis 12:1-9.

Purpose: To see how Abraham found faith to obey the Lord even without great knowledge or long experience of him.

Question 1. Abram's father Terah had moved the family from Ur, "a prosperous city with security and a high standard of living" (David Alexander and Pat Alexander, eds., *Eerdmans' Handbook to the Bible* [Grand Rapids, Mich.: Eerdmans, 1973], p. 136). They set out for Canaan but settled in Haran, which is where God called Abram (later renamed Abraham in Gen 17:5). There is no indication that Abram or Sarai knew or worshiped the Lord before Abram's call.

Question 2. Scripture does *not* tell several things: how quickly Abraham decided to leave, how soon he actually left, how he broke the news to Sarah and how she responded, how either of them felt, what opposition or support they received from others besides Lot. All we are told is that Abraham packed up and went.

Question 3. "Land, family and inheritance were among the most significant elements in ancient society. For farmers and herdsmen land was their livelihood. For city dwellers land represented their political identity. Descendants represented the future. . . . When Abram gave up his place in his father's household, he forfeited his security. He was putting his survival, his identity, his future and his security in the hands of the Lord" (John Walton et al., *The IVP Bible Background Commentary: Old Testament* [Downers Grove, Ill.: InterVarsity Press, 2000], p. 43). "Abram had nothing to go on except the promise of God. But he went forth with what little guidance he had. In the years ahead he learned the absolute faithfulness and enduring friendship of God. He needed all those years to grow in that friendship—to trust it—experiencing its reality in times when he did not trust" (Lloyd John Ogilvie, *Lord of the Impossible* [Nashville: Abingdon, 1984], p. 19).

Question 4. The promise that all people would be blessed through Abraham came through direct genealogical lineage and "came to its complete realization in Christ" (E. F. Kevan, in *The New Bible Commentary,* ed. F. Davidson [Grand Rapids, Mich.: Eerdmans, 1953], p. 88).

Question 5. It could not have been a simple move. Abraham was seventy-five years old, and Sarah was ten years younger (Gen 17:17). Their destination was unclear. They took along all their possessions, which included herds of livestock such as sheep, goats, cattle, camels and donkeys. They also took "the people they had acquired in Haran," which meant servants and some family members, at least Lot and his family. It would have been hard to explain their action to people in Haran, particularly to relatives in that culture where clans traditionally stayed together, and especially to people who did not know this God.

Question 6. In the group discussion time, group members described changes in which they believed they were led by God. This question gets more specific about their experiences. Group members are asked to identify how they were encouraged by God's promises.

Question 7. The route of Abraham's journey was along the Fertile Crescent through what is now Iraq, Syria, Lebanon and Israel. It was a well-traveled route of trade and conquest.

Question 10. In Christian hymns, Canaan sometimes symbolizes heaven because it was the Promised Land. As the Israelites crossed the Jordan River into Canaan after the exodus and wilderness wanderings (Josh 3), we will cross the Jordan of physical death and enter heaven. However, because the Israelites lived among the Canaanites and often fell under their idolatrous influence, Canaan also symbolizes the worldly ways of nonbelievers.

Question 12. Twice it says that Abraham built an altar to the Lord; the second time it adds that he also called on the name of the Lord. Altars appear in the worship of all kinds of gods and could take various forms, but they were always raised structures on which to make offerings to a god. Abraham's altars were probably simple structures such as a large rock or a pile of stones (Harold M. Wiener, "Altar," in *The International Standard Bible Encyclopedia,* vol. 1 [Wilmington, Del.: Associated Publishers and Authors, orig. 1915], p. 107). "Altars function as sacrificial platforms. Their construction can also mark the introduction of the worship of a particular god in a new land. Abram's setting up of altars in each place where he camped defines areas to be occupied in the 'Promised Land' and establishes these places as religious centers in later periods" (Walton, *IVP Bible Background Commentary: Old Testament,* p. 44).

Study 3. Righteousness by Faith. Romans 3:19-26.

Purpose: To present the need to respond in faith to Christ's death on the cross.

Question 2. Some possibilities: regular church attendance, helping others, serving in the church, giving money to people in need, sacrificing comfort or wealth, living a good moral life. These activities are commendable when they are done out of love for God and love for others (Mt 22:37-39); however, they can also spring from superiority, pride, self-righteousness or a desire to look good to other people.

Question 3. One of the most difficult admissions we can make is that we are powerless to earn approval from God. Our good works cannot negate or compensate for our sins. "The Jews are the ones specifically 'under the law' whether this refers to the law as given to Moses or the whole Old Testament. . . . [T]he Gentiles without having the advantage of the law as given to the Jews were still guilty of the things outlined in the law and come under the same condemnation. The solidarity of the human race is to be seen not only in its common bondage to sin but its common guilt before the law of God" (D. Stuart Briscoe, *The Communicator's Commentary: Romans* [Waco, Tex.: Word, 1985], p. 84).

Question 4. God's law is the perfect standard that shows us how imperfect we are. It reveals God's holiness. It exposes our sin. It stops all excuses and all boasting before God. In Galatians 3:24, Paul writes that "the law was put in charge to lead us to Christ that we might be justified by faith." "Put in charge" translates the Greek word *paidagogos*, literally "child-leader." It refers to a slave who had special responsibility for a child. "The slave assigned to this role would watch out for the student on his way to school and help him with his manners and schoolwork, but he was not the teacher himself"(Keener, *IVP Bible Background Commentary: New Testament*, p. 528).

Question 7. The verb *atone* and noun *atonement* (v. 25) come from the English words "at one." They refer to the means of reconciliation after a wrong is done. The "sacrifice of atonement" (v. 25) refers to Old Testament animal offerings for sin, both daily (Ex 29:36) and on the annual Day of Atonement (Lev 16). By his death Christ has become the once-and-for-all sacrifice which reconciles God and humanity (Heb 10:10-12). Instead of humanity offering an insufficient sacrifice for sin, God—the one who had been sinned against— presented his Son as the perfect sacrifice. God is the one who does the justifying. He does it not because anyone compels him but freely by his grace.

Question 8. Faith in Christ is the only appropriate response to what God has done in him. His death on the cross is not an example to strive for or a goad to make us work harder. It is an invitation to faith. When we trust Christ, his sacrificial death removes our offense before God.

"When I was in training as a Marine, I remember one particularly grueling exercise where we were deposited in the center of Dartmoor, one of the bleakest parts of England, and told to make our way on foot to a certain point on the map more than fifty rugged miles away. . . . [My partner] came to the point of admitting he was through, and then I was able to pick him up, put him across my shoulders, and carry him the rest of the way. He had no option but to trust himself to me to do for him what he was incapable of doing for himself. It was hard for him to be so humiliated, but it was his sole recourse, and it is hard for proud people like Paul and other earnest people to admit that there is no way of justification through self-effort, but only through 'faith in Jesus Christ'" (Briscoe, *Romans,* pp. 90-91).

Question 9. "'Redemption' (freeing a slave) was a standard Old Testament concept; the Old Testament terms always involve the paying of a price, sometimes to get something back. God 'redeemed' Israel, making them his people by grace and by paying a price for their freedom (the Passover lamb and the firstborn of Egypt), before he gave them his commandments (cf. Ex 20:2). In Paul's day, the Jewish people were looking forward to the messianic redemption, when they would be delivered from earthly rulers; but the malevolent ruler here is sin (3:9)" (Keener, *IVP Bible Background Commentary: New Testament,* pp. 420-21).

Group members may give safe, generalized answers to this question. If you think they will respond well, ask this further question: "From what types of slavery has Christ delivered you?" This is a good place to point out that, later in Romans, Paul says we are freed from slavery to sin in order to become slaves of righteousness (Rom 6:15-23). At the beginning of this letter Paul introduces himself as the servant (literally slave) of Christ (Rom 1:1).

Question 10. If time allows, you could add the following comment and question to the study: "According to John 2:23-24, certain people saw Jesus' miraculous signs and believed in him. Jesus, however, was skeptical of their faith because he knew what was inside them. How would you explain the difference between the apparently nonsaving faith of those people and the saving faith in Romans?"

There is an important difference between the two kinds of "faith." Many of us spend years believing in Jesus as great teacher, miracle worker or religious leader. We affirm the facts about him and admire him, but we still assume we are connected with God by our own moral rightness. Then we come to realize that we are not only morally insufficient but are in sinful rebellion against God. We realize our only hope is to believe in Christ in the sense of trusting him to forgive our sin and reconcile us to God. Then our belief becomes a matter of resting our entire lives on him (as in Romans) rather than affirming certain truths about him (as in John).

Question 11. Note again how throughout this passage Paul emphasizes the initiative and action of God. God has done something we can believe and has given us someone we can trust. Accept the salvation he is offering you, and accept his assurance that you are forgiven.

Study 4. Naaman: Faith Without Fireworks. 2 Kings 5:1-15.

Purpose: To see the effectiveness of a simple act of faith in God.

Question 1. "The land of Aram, north of the land of Israel, was known by the Greeks as Syria. Current evidence suggests that the Arameans inhabited the upper Euphrates throughout the second millennium [B.C.], first as villagers and pastoralists, then as a political, national coalition. During this period they are alternately allies and the most troublesome foes of Israel" (Walton, *IVP Bible Background Commentary: Old Testament*, p. 390).

The term *leprosy* could refer to any eruptive skin disease. While the Jews had various laws of uncleanness and purification in regard to leprosy, it appears that there was no particular stigma attached to it in Syria (Aram). "In Syria, leprosy caused only physical incapacity to perform required duties; Naaman as a leper won no further victories for Syria, and this caused genuine concern" (Harold Stigers, *The Wycliffe Bible Commentary* [Nashville: Southwestern, 1962], p. 345).

Question 2. It was on one of Aram's frequent border raids against Israel that a young Jewish girl was captured and became slave to Naaman's wife. "The prophet who is in Samaria" (v. 3) is Elisha. Scripture records even more miracles by Elisha than by his predecessor Elijah. The young girl had heard of Elisha's miracles (2 Kings 3—4) and perhaps had even seen him at work. It is touching to see this unnamed girl's empathy for the commander of the soldiers who stole her from her homeland—especially when we consider that he owned her as a piece of property.

Question 4. The tearing of robes was a sign of mourning. The king of Israel at this time was apparently Joram, son of the infamous Ahab (2 Kings 3:1). He was later killed by Jehu while recovering from wounds he received in a battle with the king of Aram (2 Kings 9:14-15).

Question 7. "Since Elisha is probably in Samaria, . . . the trip to the Jordan would have been about forty miles. There is no easy, direct route from Samaria to the Jordan. He probably would have gone back the way he came: north to Dothan, through the Dothan Valley to the Valley of Jezreel, from Jezreel through the Gilboa pass to Beth Shan and then on to the Jordan" (Walton, *IVP Bible Background Commentary: Old Testament*, p. 391).

Question 12. The chief god of Syria was Rimmon, god of storms and thunder. Naaman customarily accompanied his master, the king of Syria, to the temple of Rimmon to worship. It was a huge step for Naaman to renounce Rimmon and all the lesser gods of his country and to confess that "there is no God in all the world except in Israel." We know he meant that Israel's God is the only God, not simply that God was localized in Israel, for Naaman asked for a load of earth to take back with him to make an altar to the Lord. He also begged a special indulgence to bow down in apparent worship of Rimmon when the king of Syria, leaning on his arm, bowed down to the idol (vv. 17-18).

Study 5. Faith Without Action. James 2:14-26.
Purpose: To understand the intersection of faith and action, and to evaluate the health of our own faith.
Group discussion. If time allows and you want to go deeper, you might follow up with, "When are you tempted to exaggerate, and why?"
General note. If you are curious about who James is, the evidence is that this letter was written by "James, the Lord's brother" (see Gal 1:19).
Question 2. What is this dead "faith" which James condemns? By itself, verse 14 implies that faith is not enough for salvation and must be supplemented with deeds. Salvation through deeds contradicts the doctrine of salvation by faith in Christ which runs throughout the New Testament (see study three). When James asks "Can such faith save him?" (v. 14) the implied answer is "No, of course not." Such non-saving "faith" is not genuine faith at all.
Question 7. The gospels give evidence that demons acknowledge Jesus as the Son of God but do not willingly submit to his lordship. When Jesus confronted a demon-possessed man in the synagogue at Capernaum, the demon cried out, "I know who you are—the Holy One of God!" (Lk 4:34). Later he cast out other evil spirits who shouted, "You are the Son of God!" (Lk 4:41). The man possessed by a legion of demons cried out "What do you want with me, Jesus, Son of the Most High God?"(Mk 5:7). The demons believe the facts of who Jesus is, but they still serve Satan rather than God.
Question 8. In study 2 you read about the beginnings of Abraham's faith in the Lord. The story of Abraham's willingness to sacrifice his promised son Isaac is found in Genesis 22. Verse 23 quotes Genesis 15:6, after God promised Abraham that his descendants would be as many as the stars. Rahab concealed the spies who investigated Jericho when Israel was about to invade Canaan. She told them she believed that the Lord was the true God. For her actions, her life and the lives of her family were spared (Josh 2; 6:22-23).
Question 9. In this passage James has argued that a claim to faith without works is only empty words. "The emptiness of such profession is not new in the NT. One has only to scan the prophets to discover a condemnation of ritual piety without practical justice for the poor. . . . John the Baptist is also reported as demanding deeds be added to faith (Luke 3:7-14), and Jesus warned that it would not do to enter the last judgment merely verbalizing his lordship (Matthew 7:15-27; cf. 5:16). Paul also reiterates this theme (Romans

1:5; 2:6-8; 6:17-18; 1 Corinthians 13:2; 15:28; 2 Corinthians 10:5-6; Galatians 6:4-6). . . . Works are not an 'added extra' to faith, but are an essential expression of it" (Peter H. Davids, *Commentary on James,* New International Greek Testament Commentary [Grand Rapids, Mich.: Eerdmans, 1982], pp. 120-21).

These further thoughts will help shed light on the different emphases of Paul and James: "James and Paul are moving in two different worlds. In James's world Jewish ritual is not an issue (perhaps because all of those in his church are Jews), but ethics is. His problems are with those who claim to be right with God on the basis of their orthodoxy although they are ignoring obedience issues, especially charity. Abraham and Rahab, in contrast to the demons, demonstrate that saving faith is seen in its deeds. Paul, on the other hand, is concerned about the relationship of Jews and Gentiles in the church. His concern is that commitment to Jesus as Lord is all that is necessary for salvation. A Gentile does not have to become a Jew to enter the kingdom; those ritual deeds that marked the Jew are unnecessary. In the places were Paul does address the issue of whether a person can enter the kingdom while living in sin, he emphatically denies this is possible, agreeing with James" (Walter C. Kaiser Jr. et al., *Hard Sayings of the Bible* [Downers Grove, Ill.: InterVarsity Press, 1996], pp. 698-99).

Question 10. Group members may hesitate to give examples because they don't wish to brag. You could restate the question this way: "Where do you *hope* people see evidences of authentic faith in Christ?" Some group members may volunteer evidences for other group members who are hesitant. The "Now or Later" activity gives all of you the opportunity to affirm each other's goods works in Christ.

Study 6. David: Faith That Worships. 2 Samuel 7:18-29.
Purpose: To demonstrate how faith leads naturally into worship.
Question 1. This Scripture passage does not reveal the reasons God denied David the privilege of building the temple. Later, when David charges his son Solomon to build the temple, he explains: "But this word of the LORD came to me: 'You have shed much blood and have fought many wars. You are not to build a house for my Name, because you have shed much blood on the earth in my sight'" (1 Chron 22:8). Solomon, by contrast, would be a man of peace. Apparently this revelation came to David directly and not through Nathan.
Question 2. To go in and sit before the Lord (v. 18) could mean that David went into the tabernacle or that he simply went someplace where he was accustomed to praying. This was not the only instance that David turned to the Lord in worship at a difficult time. Many of David's psalms were written under great

stress, danger or frustration, yet they consistently express faith that is strengthened in worship. Some striking examples are Psalms 28, 31, 35 and 38.

Question 3. David used the same construction in Psalm 8: "What is man that
you are mindful of him, the son of man that you care for him?" (Ps 8:4). The
question is an expression of wonder that God takes such an interest in weak,
unworthy human beings.

Question 8. David freely asked for God's favor on himself and his house. Yet
his prayer was not that he and his descendants would have great renown, but
that the whole world would know that the God of Israel is the only God.
David prayed that "the house of your servant David will be established *before
you*" (v. 26), that it "may continue forever *in your sight*" (v. 29) and that "*with
your blessing* the house of your servant will be blessed forever" (v. 29). The
line of David would endure, not through any merit of its own, but because it
was established by the Lord.

Question 9. There is no particular right answer to this question. Let group
members identify which of David's words speak to them most strongly of his
faith. Members are likely to focus on the words that come closest to their own
situations.

Study 7. The Focus of Faith. Hebrews 12:1-11.

Purpose: To clear away distractions and focus on Jesus Christ.

Questions 2-3. For many of us, the whole of life feels like a race! We hurry
from one responsibility to the next, and church activities may only contribute
to the frantic pace. The "race marked out for us" is not the rat race of an over-
scheduled life. The word translated "race" also means "conflict," both inward
and outward. The Christian's life in pursuit of Christlikeness is a battle
against internal and external forces that try to drag us backward.

Question 4. "With the great gallery of witnesses about us, it is important for
us to run well. So we are exhorted, 'Let us throw off everything that hinders.'
'Everything that hinders' translates *onkos* (only here in the New Testament), a
word that means any kind of weight. It is sometimes used of superfluous
body weight that the athlete sheds during training. Here, however, it seems to
be the race rather than the training that is in view. Athletes carried nothing
with them in a race (they even ran naked), and the writer is suggesting that
the Christian should 'travel light.' He is not referring to sin, for that follows in
the next clause. Some things that are not wrong in themselves hinder us in
putting forward our best effort. So the writer tells us to get rid of them" (Leon
Morris, *The Expositor's Bible Commentary,* ed. Frank E. Gaebelein [Grand Rapids, Mich.: Zondervan, 1981], pp. 133-34).

Question 7. First Peter 2:21-24 gives a moving summary of Christ as our example of perseverance under suffering.

Questions 8-9. "In the context of Jewish wisdom literature, discipline was a sign of a father's love for his children, his concern that they would go in the right way. . . . In the Greek world, the term translated 'discipline' . . . was the most basic term for 'education' (although this usually included corporal discipline), so the term naturally conveyed the concept of moral instruction. Some philosophers like Seneca also used the image of God disciplining his children for their good, just as Jewish writers did. In antiquity, calling someone an 'illegitimate child' . . . was a grievous insult; illegitimacy negatively affected one's social status as well as one's inheritance rights. Fathers were more concerned for their heirs and usually invested little time in illegitimate sons" (Keener, *IVP Bible Background Commentary: New Testament*, p. 679).

Question 12. "The Christian . . . is not a tourist, who returns each night to the place from which he started; he is a pilgrim who is for ever on the way. The goal is nothing less than Christ Himself, the presence of Christ, the likeness of Christ. The Christian life is going somewhere, and it would be well if, at each day's ending, we were to ask ourselves: 'Am I any farther on?'" (Barclay, *Letter to the Hebrews*, p. 195).

Study 8. In Jesus' Name: Faith That Asks. John 16:16-28.

Purpose: To consider the meaning and the right occasions of praying in Jesus' name.

Question 2. A listener's mood would no doubt change as Jesus said difficult things and gave reassurance—while still not answering every question.

Question 3. Point out the context of these words of Jesus. It was his last evening with his disciples before he would be crucified. He knew he was about to die. They should have known it because he had told them (Mt 20:17-19), but they had forgotten or denied it. Jesus had been the object of their loyalty, even worship, for three years. How could he talk of leaving them?

Question 4. Jesus did not specifically answer the disciples' questions. He did not mention the cross, resurrection or heaven. Instead of an explanation, he gave them a promise: that their separation from him would be temporary, and their reunion would be forever.

Question 5. In a culture where children were born at home in small houses, childbirth was a familiar event. The disciples would experience suffering when Jesus left, but they would come through their suffering and would see its purpose. Their pain would be fruitful, resulting in life and joy.

Question 8. It is important to steer group members away from the idea that the words "in Jesus' name" are a sort of spiritual lever by which we can move God to do what we want. "In Jesus' name" is not a magical formula. The power of prayer in the name of Jesus lies not in the words themselves but in our intent to ask only what the Son of God would ask. The following comments will be helpful: "Jesus is the Lord incarnate, and thus he himself bears this divine name. He is not simply a courier of revelation like Moses. He is revelation. Jesus' own name has power and significance, . . . and thus prayer uttered in his name will witness results. . . . But the power of prayer in Jesus' name resides in the fact that, as 14:13 shows, the Father himself is being glorified through Jesus" (G. M. Burge, in Dictionary of Jesus and the Gospels, ed. Joel B. Green and Scot McKnight [Downers Grove, Ill.: InterVarsity Press, 1992], p. 356).

"In the Old Testament 'name' often meant reputation or renown, and when God acted 'on account of his name' it was to defend his honor. . . . In this context [Jesus' words] 'name' means something like: those who seek his glory and speak accurately for him, who are genuinely his authorized representatives. Nothing could be further from the pagan magical use of names that sought to manipulate spiritual forces for one's own ends" (Keener, IVP Bible Background Commentary: New Testament, p. 300).

Study 9. The Finale of Faith. 2 Timothy 4:6-18.
Purpose: To draw hope from the assurance that Christ will be faithful to the end.
Question 2. Notice that Paul compares his life to a race. Remind group members of the "race marked out for us" from Hebrews 12:1 in study 7.

Paul's statement that he is already being poured out like a drink offering (v. 6) fulfills his expectation in Philippians 2:17, where he expected his life to be poured out like a drink offering on the faith of the Philippians. In the Jewish law, the daily sacrifice included a drink offering of wine poured onto the daily burnt offering of a lamb (Ex 29:38-41).

Concerning Paul's colorful imagery in verses 6-7: "Paul's first image is the athletic contest, probably wrestling in the arena; moralists commonly borrowed this image to describe struggles on behalf of virtue. . . . 'Completed the course' refers to a race, again popular athletic imagery. 'Keeping faith' was a Greek expression for loyalty, similar to a Hebrew expression meaning remaining faithful to the covenant, or in some cases, guarding the true faith (thus 'the faith' here)" (Keener, IVP Bible Background Commentary: New Testament, p. 631).

The lion's mouth (v. 17) could be both literal and figurative. Paul died during the persecution under the Roman emperor Nero, when Christians were literally thrown to the lions, although he escaped that fate. The prophet Daniel was miraculously kept alive in a den of lions (Dan 6). During his time as a shepherd, King David killed lions (1 Sam 17:34-37). Peter compared the devil to a roaring lion who seeks someone to devour (1 Pet 5:8).

Question 5. Mark is undoubtedly John Mark, who accompanied Paul and Barnabas on mission journeys and whose departure caused a split between the two (Acts 13:1-13; 15:36-39). Mark became the gospel writer. By summoning him to help, Paul shows that he had overcome his old disappointment with Mark and accepted him as a partner. The scrolls and parchments are "possibly copies of Old Testament books, Paul's own notebooks, or personal papers" (*Eerdmans' Handbook*, p. 622). Expecting to die soon, Paul looked toward the future and called for the people and materials that would make the foundation of a continuing witness.

Question 6. The imminence of death brings all of Paul's relationships, both good and bad, into sharp focus. He now has no doubts about who his friends and opponents are. He longs to see Timothy; he is reconciled with Mark; he feels abandoned by Demas; he leaves Alexander to God's justice; he misses Crescens, Titus, Tychicus and many others; he holds fast to Luke's faithfulness.

Questions 7-8. It comforts us to know that even Paul, who said "I can do everything through him who gives me strength" (Phil 4:13), experienced disappointment with people, and the feeling did not immediately go away. He stood fast only because "the Lord stood at my side and gave me strength."

Question 10. From the very beginning, Paul was marked out to carry the gospel to the Gentiles—non-Jewish people who were not looking for the Jewish Messiah. Christ described Paul (then Saul) as "my chosen instrument to carry my name before the Gentiles" (Acts 9:15). Paul called himself "the apostle to the Gentiles" (Rom 11:13).

Dale and Sandy Larsen are writers living in Greenville, Illinois. They have authored over thirty Bible studies, including the LifeGuide® Bible Study Hosea: God's Persistent Love.

What Should We Study Next?

A good place to continue your study of Scripture would be with a book study. Many groups begin with a Gospel such as *Mark* (20 studies by Jim Hoover) or *John* (26 studies by Douglas Connelly). These guides are divided into two parts so that if twenty or twenty-six weeks seems like too much to do at once, the group can feel free to do half and take a break with another topic. Later you might want to come back to it. You might prefer to try a shorter letter. *Philippians* (9 studies by Donald Baker), *Ephesians* (11 studies by Andrew T. and Phyllis J. Le Peau) and *1 & 2 Timothy and Titus* (11 studies by Pete Sommer) are good options. If you want to vary your reading with an Old Testament book, consider *Ecclesiastes* (12 studies by Bill and Teresa Syrios) for a challenging and exciting study.

There are a number of interesting topical LifeGuide studies as well. Here are some options for filling three or four quarters of a year:

Basic Discipleship
Christian Beliefs, 12 studies by Stephen D. Eyre
Christian Character, 12 studies by Andrea Sterk & Peter Scazzero
Christian Disciplines, 12 studies by Andrea Sterk & Peter Scazzero
Evangelism, 12 studies by Rebecca Pippert & Ruth Siemens

Building Community
Fruit of the Spirit, 9 studies by Hazel Offner
Spiritual Gifts, 12 studies by Charles & Anne Hummel
Christian Community, 10 studies by Rob Suggs

Character Studies
David, 12 studies by Jack Kuhatschek
New Testament Characters, 10 studies by Carolyn Nystrom
Old Testament Characters, 12 studies by Peter Scazzero
Women of the Old Testament, 12 studies by Gladys Hunt

The Trinity
Meeting God, 12 studies by J. I. Packer
Meeting Jesus, 13 studies by Leighton Ford
Meeting the Spirit, 10 studies by Douglas Connelly